ALSO BY VIRGINIA HAMILTON ADAIR

Ants on the Melon
Beliefs and Blasphemies

LIVING ON FIRE

LIVING
ON FIRE

A Collection of Poems

VIRGINIA HAMILTON ADAIR

RANDOM HOUSE

NEW YORK

Copyright © 2000 by Virginia Hamilton Adair

All rights reserved under International and
Pan-American Copyright Conventions. Published in
the United States by Random House, Inc., New York,
and simultaneously in Canada by Random House
of Canada Limited, Toronto.

RANDOM HOUSE and colophon are
registered trademarks of Random House, Inc.

"Crime Passionnel" was originally published, in slightly
different form, as "New Patient on Men's Receiving" in the
Summer 1970 issue of *Massachusetts Review,*
Vol. XI, number 3.

Library of Congress Cataloging-in-Publication Data

Adair, Virginia, 1913–
Living on fire : a collection of poems / Virginia Hamilton Adair.—1st ed.
        p.   cm.
ISBN 0-375-50289-0 (alk. paper)
I. Title.
PS3551.D244 L58 2000
811'.54—dc21   99-052858

Random House website address www.atrandom.com
Printed in the United States of America on acid-free paper

24689753

FIRST EDITION

To Nancy Ware,
whose generous weekend sessions
helped this book to come alive

Two decades of my youth, I lived on fire,
trapped in a deep delirium of desire.
I was the spirit's wastrel and a fool,
and I have taken fifty years to cool.

Contents

PART I

GENERATIONS

An Hour in Aldwinkle

Dryden, whose name and wit an age adorn,
beside a nameless and deserted lane,
we found your grandsire's tiny church forlorn,
open to bird and beast, to wind and rain,
where farmers stored their tools and sacks of grain.

This place where centuries had heard the Mass
was now with birds' graffiti stippled white,
but under broken bench and shards of glass
glimmered a fine medieval funeral brass.
We pushed the trash aside and brushed it bright.

Our search for Dryden landmarks, I confess,
stopped with this neighbor from an earlier age,
with tonsured head and simple knee-length dress.
William, of unknown deeds and lineage,
still looked heroic on his humble stage.

His eyes on some vast promise seemed to feed,
impervious to fate and time's attacks.
In homage more than mere collector's greed,

we knelt amid the bird and rodent tracks
to trace his effigy in cobbler's wax.

A star or two began to blur and twinkle
through rifts in England's overlay of cloud,
before we raised up William of Aldwinkle
and bore him with us in his paper shroud.
Brass rubbing at that time was still allowed.

But what a place to find a brass to rub!
Aldwinkle didn't even have a pub.

The Names

Ten generations back, and the family legends fall
into oblivion. A company of names we still recall:
Keller, Armstrong, Taylor, Cook,
inscriptions in the Holy Book.
Lives of glory, and of shame,
giving the newborn slave his name.
Dr. Hopson's bearded face
hanging by the mantlepiece,
Gwathmey, Hamilton, Lewis, Clark,
two who mapped the wilderness
of their country's endless park.
Scouts, explorers, soldiers, friends,
Meriwether's story ends
in mystery on the Natchez Trace.
Browning, Bullit, Berry, Bell,
a bit of yellowed wedding lace,
a flower from the Holy Land,
picked by a pilgrim's long dead hand.
Of all, so little left to tell,
too little left to know them well,
hardly surviving, if at all,

a snuffbox or a pipe,
in portrait or daguerreotype.
And still their music boxes chime
the hit tunes of an older time;
and still a family presence hovers, though unseen,
over the silver ladle, tray, and soup tureen.

Hard to Die

Meriwether Lewis and his men tracked a wounded bear
to its deathbed gouged under a bush by its great claws,
and gave it a final bullet to the brain.

"Hard to die," wrote Lewis,
of the grizzlies killed by his men on the way west.
And "hard to die," he wrote of himself
a few years later before his death—
shot, we assume, by his own hand,
alone in some sad passion or despondency
on the Natchez Trace.

The Great River

In the last year of my childhood
I met the Mississippi at New Orleans.
The houseboat *POLLY,* moored at the levee,
carried eight of us and a crew of five.
A child's dream cast: the captain had a hook,
the steward Charlie had a patch on one eye.

The great river seemed benign despite tales of flood.
We were shown by a priest the island where a statue
of the Virgin had three times saved the little town.
Sometimes our waterways became narrow and dim, dark
        mirrors
under live-oak branches hung with Spanish moss and snakes:
Bayou Big Pigeon, Bayou Little Pigeon, Bayou Teche.

Children rushed from shanties or came out in pirogues,
standing at the oars,
bending to get the candy and baseballs we threw them.

On Laffite's Island I scratched with a stick for pirates' treasure.
In the evenings I read forbidden books in the ship's lounge.

"Why isn't the child wearing glasses?" someone asked.
"She can hardly see."
My mother was mortified. "Don't hold the book so close,
    Virginia."

But I was in heaven on the *POLLY,*
only mildly bothered by grown-up people.
I wrote eight poems during one day.
I fished off the stern of the boat with Reed, the cabin boy.

My childhood still lingers in the secret bayous,
the soft land-and-waterscape seen without glasses,
where the great Mississippi,
even in times of flood, must never rise
above the feet of the Virgin on her small island.

Porches I

In those days the front porches
with their wicker chairs and hanging baskets of flowers
became chapels of rest at the day's end,
long arms of the setting sun reaching out to us.

Talk came in soft murmurs like a prayer.
The children gathered from their games
to sit in silence on the wooden steps.

The trees were ancient guardians around us
and the closing down of evening was like violet eyelids
lowered over the day's brightness.

"We should light the lamps," someone said.
But who would care to spoil the quiet ritual
of sundown, nightfall? Somewhere just ahead
lay the ceremony of sleep.

Porches II

All over our U.S. the porches were dying.
The porch swing and the rocking chair moved to the village
    dump.
The floorboards trembled, and the steps creaked.
For a couple of decades a new light burned in the parlor,
the family sitting there silent in front of the box,
voices and music squawking mysteriously from far places
into the dim-lit room. Conversation was hushed.

In the next two decades, a window in the box
flashed unbelievable pictures into the room.
Strangers guffawed and howled with laughter.
Shots rang out, people died in front of our eyes.
We learned not to care, drinking Coca-Cola from bottles,
spilling popcorn into the sofa.

A highway came past the house with its deserted porch
and no one noticed. The children wandered off to rob houses
a few blocks away, not out of need, but simple boredom.
No more family games or read-alouds.

Grandparents sometimes pulled their chairs outside
hoping neighbors would stop in.
They might even drag out an extra chair or two;
still no one came, not even to borrow something.
But it was hard to talk with the TV at their backs,
the traffic screeching by in front, the rest of the neighborhood
on relief, or in rest homes and reformatories.

The old porch is removed, and the grandparents with it.
So long, friends, neighbors, passersby.

Food for Thought

The ants rush about importantly,
their city flourishes under the hot sand.
A horned toad licks them up with its long tongue.

A man kneels in the sand.
He chips at a red rock with his little pick and hammer.
The emerging fossil was once a hunger, food, and motion.

The man eats a ham sandwich and meditates.
Something has gone very wrong with his species.
They multiply without mercy or meaning.
They are killing each other, but not fast enough.

He contemplates the next billion years
while the sun moves his shadow imperceptibly.
His teeth close on the pig that died for his appetite.
Staring at the fossil, he chews slowly.
He has looked into the eyes of time, and they are hostile.

PART II

NOTES AND NOISES

Notes from Another City

As you struck the keys
a force of visions and passions came forth.
I was seeing the hands of the composer
over the keyboard marking black notes on white paper.
All the while, beyond a window:
the autumn leaves were letting go,
saying good-bye to the parent tree,
the safe residence of the bough;
I could see their colors as the shaper of the sonata
saw them, winging into the water
that eddies under the stone bridge,
coloring the cobbles under the horse's hoofs,
half-heard, half-seen by the musician.
The living line under his pen marked the melody in his mind,
while its rhythm partook of the ghostly hoofbeats,
passing so long ago, so far distant.

The builder of that edifice of sounds heard it,
and the pianist of this morning
a hundred years beyond the builder's death
heard it, and I, listening as a ghost in that town

look up at the window
behind which the composer plays a bar,
watches the leaves falling and fallen,
puts their track on paper:
the white silence that will be reborn
forever at the touch of two hands.

Sonnet to Pan

Pan, I have come again through the noon heat,
letting your name resound in the quiet glade
where long ago a child came, unafraid
to lay some gift, a waving wand of wheat
or clover cluster, at your horny feet.
Then was the simple offering well repaid:
a thousand summer voices, as you played,
led by your lifted pipes, rang pure and sweet.

Now as I strain to hear the haunting sound
of careless laughter on your curving lips,
the oak burl winks; and suddenly as before,
I feel your hoofbeats lightly shake the ground;
but when I turn to look, the vision slips,
held by these nets of sun and shade no more.

Evensongs

In the days before RV's
the sound of tent pegs being driven in was music,
and the whisper, then crackle, of a wood fire
getting under way.

After the steak smells and the cleanup,
it was bliss to lie back against a log
and just listen:
an owl, announcing the evening hunt,
an unseen mother calling, Juny, Juny.
At a distance, a chord on a guitar,
a few bars on a mouth organ.

With my head on his shoulder,
my husband began to sing "St. James Infirmary"
mellow, seductive, and slightly off-key.
A song for necrophiliacs. Poe would have loved it.

Downwind we heard the harmonica and guitar
joined by a flute, feeling their way into a trio.

The owl called close by
and the darkening fire gave a long sigh,
as if falling asleep.

The Sound of Progress

The world is charged with the clangor of Hell.
     It will drum out, like thunder from shook tin;
     It gathers to a frenzy, like foul fuels within
Jets. Why do men now not check these fell
Cacophonies that so repel, repel, repel?
     For all is seared with sound, bleared, smeared with din
     That slashes through our calm like a shark's fin.
Nor can one dodge the harrowing decibel.

And for all this, noises are never spent;
     There revs the mightiest motor in all things:
Diesel and drag race down the street just went,
     Gears groan, tires shriek, the fatal siren sings—
Curst home appliances over our bent
     Ears brood and hum and madden with their stings.

Bartók

Driving one night, I felt my little car rock.
The radio and I went into star shock
while heaven and earth cried Bartók, Bartók, Bartók.
A frenzy of lovers in their mating doomed,
stamping the floors of heaven into stars,
die in the flames of passion, self-consumed.
Furious winds of space, their avatars
the earthly godlings Kali, Lucifer, Mars,
Mammon and Moloch, served by witch and warlock,
all of them screaming Bartók, Bartók, Bartók.

Rumblings

Satie said he adored his lover's belch:
a spasm which he begged her not to squelch,
a sound as swift and sharp as from a rifle,
a sound which Satie urged her not to stifle.
Beside these rumblings from his love's interior,
he felt his compositions were inferior.

Scarlatti

On the beaches of the world
Scarlatti still walks reinventing
the race of notes under his fingers
while the waves spilling over themselves shoreward
read his mind when the wind blows a certain way
writing his name in flourishes of foam
racing in time to his rhythms
telling the sand to be firm
under the master's feet.

PART III

THE FLUTED SHELL

1

Light Verse

Still

When I was two and twenty
with highlights in my hair,
I lived to love, my darlings,
and love was everywhere.

Now I am two and eighty
and snow is on the hill,
but age is not so weighty
for love surrounds me still.

Echoes

Evelyn of Fall River, newly in love,
forgot her mom's complaints,
the vacuum cleaner's whine,
and the smells of supper.
As she rose and fell, under her lover's weight,
she shed the sorrows of her childhood,
entering a new life.

O you grown old,
working the wheelchair down the hall,
remember your first passion, and pity Evelyn,
who will someday be shapeless and incontinent
even as you, witless, wasted, and unwanted
by a world of strangers.

Cavy Family

Our guinea pigs were lovers to the last;
they had sex often and they had it fast.
He hugged her furry loins to raise his length;
she kept on eating to keep up her strength.
With numerous young the guinea god did bless her,
each litter larger than its predecessor.
The guinea piglets came at birth complete;
they groomed their whiskers and began to eat.

In Williamsburg their memory still survives:
how dogs broke in and took their harmless lives,
the little corpses with pink ears and feet
strewn up and down the Duke of Gloucester Street.
For you, whose ways so often made us laugh,
near tears, I type this woeful epitaph.

Marital Love

"How do I love thee? Let me count the ways."
The effort took Miss Barrett several days,
resulting in a book of amorous lays,
when wives were weak behind their whalebone stays.
And did she yawn and smilingly endure
as Robert's verse got more and more obscure?

Old Pickup

bent body
scarred
rotting inside

driven dry
parts hanging down
eroded &

unscrewed

turned over once
rattled &
died

Hetaera McMurdo

My father leaning forward
fingered her buttons like a man
with a huge mistress. She sang to him,
whispered in Russian, Portuguese, and French,
brought him, with dizzy cackles,
tidbits from Montreal and Rome.

Creation too ingenious for her time,
she could change records, slinging them
down a velvet ramp: recordings made
at 33⅓ r.p.m., unheard of then. *The Swan
of Tuonela* played for twenty minutes.
"So what's the point?" friends asked.

At midnight Mother called, "Come up to bed!"
But still he lingered with his mammoth love.
In Berlin it was already tomorrow
and multilingual McMurdo stopped a polka
to treat my father to a bloodbath,
while hero Hitler waited in the wings.

Soon she would toss nations down her ramp,
make maps run wild at 33⅓ r.p.m.
Through World War II, Korea, and Vietnam
she made him see it all with his two ears.
How could the local TV tart compete
with one who roamed the shortwaves of the world?

My father, faithful to their long tryst,
carried her with him across the continent,
replaced her archaic tubes and coils,
trying for Tokyo. Forty years beyond
der Führer's purge, his last gaze
caressed the giant form facing his bed.

Venice Beach

You, Aphrodite in ebony, seven feet tall,
going by on roller blades, boom box blaring,
the Pacific Ocean beyond its acres of sand
is small beside you.

Prouder than Nubian queens,
Cleopatra, or all the wives of Solomon,
you swoop like the mythic bird
that bore away Sinbad.

You are the stuff of the new world,
emerging from its racist and intemperate history,
with song, dance, and laughter.
Do not be paranoid

about Great-Grandma's bondage;
white grandmas, too, were slaves to this and that,
morals and manners that never hampered you,
traveling tall to an arrogant drumbeat,

dwarfing the breakers in your personal waves
of sound and speed, speed and sound,
one with the wind and a world waiting
for your roller blades and a black sunrise.

2

Young Love

Paper Dolls

Don't you grieve none, Hattie tells me,
Miss Miriam a young lady now. Hair up. Long skirt.
No more paper dolls on the porch.

At night I hear the Victrola across the street
where Miriam waits at the door for Toby.
They hug and go inside, but I see their shadows
dancing behind the closed blinds.
The music is about smiles that make you happy
but I feel on the edge of tears.

The mother of Miriam likes Toby too.
Miriam is not allowed to go to Toby's nightclub,
where he plays his horn, but one night, watching, I see
Miriam's mother run out and jump in Toby's car.
Another time the dancers behind the blinds are Toby
and Miriam's mother. Miriam comes over, tells me
her mother wants to stay young. I ask, "Young enough
to play paper dolls?" Miriam smiles, but as the song
goes on to say, there are smiles that make you sad.

Toby's mother is talking to my mother.
I hear her say, "I could kill that slut."
Mother closes the door, and I see Miriam
coming home from high school. I run across the street
though I have been forbidden to do so.
"What is a slut, and why does Toby's mother
want to shoot one?" "Nobody," says Miriam,
"can talk that way about my mother."
She hardly seems to see me. She was happier
when she and I were playing on the porch.

Soon things become very solemn.
Miriam's mother is in the hospital, but they are not
cutting off her leg, or taking out her tonsils.
I hear the word overdose, probably castor oil.
After the funeral, Miriam's father comes by.
"Thank you for the flowers," he says.
"She wanted to be young forever."
"Now you can dance again with Toby,"
I say to Miriam. She gives me a fierce look.
"I never want to dance again," she says.
"But you said you were going to be a dancer.
Remember the paper doll in the ballet dress?"

Toby has gone to visit his grandfather.
He is playing his horn in another city,
and his mother is moving away.
In her piled-up belongings is the stuffed head of an animal,
showing its teeth. It used to hang on their wall.
"Is that the slut you shot yourself?" I ask.
But Toby's mother is deaf, and does not answer.
Besides, the van has started to carry everything away.

Hattie asks me, "Why you put all your paper dollies
in the wastebasket?" "That's the hospital," I tell her,
"they all took an overdose. And the ballerina,
they cut off her leg." "You come with me," says Hattie.
"Help me shell the peas for supper."

The Caller

After the Lutheran service and the Sunday meal,
the roast was left out to cool.
A pale island of fat lay on the shallow lake of blood.
Barbara, the visiting child, wanted to nap.
Now we will pay some calls, said Grandmother,
sad and stern (unlike the merry grannies in children's books).
"Will there be children?" asked Barbara.
"Children and babies, yes," said Grandmother in her joyless
        voice,
"two or three and many infants, and friends, old friends
who were once young and are still dear to me."
Barbara put on her coat, yawning.

The November sun was low in the sky when they set out
in the old Pontiac. The driver was an uncle who rarely spoke.
A dark cloud hung over the edge of town.
They drove on narrow empty roads
bordered by bare November fields,
a stripped tree now and then,
vine-draped like a preacher in a torn gown.
They drove past empty villages,

past little stores and scattered houses,
through places with names like Grand Meadow and
        Brownsdale,
past towns with closed doors,
all with a locked and lifeless Sunday look.

The driver slowed the car, shifted gears,
and bumped up a narrow rutted cowpath
leading to a forsaken church like a dollhouse
where all the dolls were long ago lost or broken.
The little girl trembled with cold and something else.
Where did these invisible people live
with the two or three children and many babies?
She whispered, "I'll stay in the car."

Grandmother closed the car door softly,
as if fearful of waking someone. She walked alone
through the weeds, slowly past the deserted church
into the graveyard of leaning, cracked, and fallen stones,
some with a cross, or an angel, some tilting like people
walking into the wind. The church, too, slanted into the wind,
while crows flew up like frightened choristers.
The bent figure placed a dried flower on first one grave
and then another, pausing as if to greet, pray, or reminisce.
When Grandmother came back to the car, she said
with her twisted smile, "My friends wait for me here."

The travelers drove on down the road, passing another lifeless
        town.
They stopped at a second church, a mile or so beyond,
where an iron fence stood between the headstones and the
        road.

"You have no flowers left," said Barbara.

"No," said Grandmother; "but I bring something better."

Painfully she climbed the bank, through tufts of withered
        grass,

stood at the iron fence with her head bowed.

The silent driver helped her back down the slope and into the
        car.

"I brought forgiveness," she said, as if to herself.

"It has been a hard gift to bring, after all these years."

They turned off the road toward the last churchyard.

The church had vanished, suggested only by fallen walls

and a tangle of vine. The ghost of a graveyard seemed to float

in the fading light. Grandmother walked to the edge

and touched a still-standing stone.

She took from her coat pocket something white

and tore it into tiny pieces that fluttered free from her hand.

Low in the sky, the black cloud that had followed them

was pierced by a thin bar of sunlight. A few flakes of snow

fluttered toward the old figure as she came back to the car.

She put out her bare hand as if to receive the flakes.

"This time he has answered my letter," she said.

And for an instant her face had a young girl's radiance.

Fairy Tale

The gazebo arches over her like a lover.
Against its column of pink marble
she leans her cheek.

In a sudden shower of rain she drops her gown,
rushes bare and shivering with pleasure
across the shining grass toward, of course,
a rainbow arching at the end of the garden.

A laughter of freed birds darts around her,
encircles her as she puts up her hands
to catch and stop the ribbons of the rain.

Pink worms emerge from the garden earth;
they levitate on the edge of the lily pond.

This is the dream of the girl who wakes in damp straw.
The sky puts on its monocle of sun,
its long rays touching the rivulets
along the girl's back and the ringlets in her hair.

An albino crow paces among the rosy worms,
pecking, full of purpose, perhaps
a bewitched minstrel or eligible prince.

We trust the beggar girl will disenchant
the royal lover in her next dream,
and all the worms will dance at their wedding.

Late Afternoon

The sun has gone down,
pulling the warm day with it behind the maples,
almost leafless now.
We stand by the mailbox, talking.
Flobo is a year older than I, a doctor's daughter.
After a pause, I say,
"My parents would never do such a thing."
Flobo says kindly, "They all do it.
Come over tomorrow after school;
I'll show you the pictures in Dad's medical books."

We part and I walk slowly by the long brick wall.
I begin to run and do not speak to the old lamplighter
raising his pole up to the gaslight.
At our gray-and-white front steps I stop and sit down,
pretending to tie my shoe.
Suddenly I feel ashamed to enter my own house.
Like the leaves on the sidewalk
under the gas streetlight, I feel cold and homeless.
All at once it seems sad for the leaves
never to return to their safe place along the bough.

Crime Passionnel

down the long and bare
                    (like burned over
                                    with stumps of men)
boardfloor gouged sullied splintered ammoniac
                    one corpse   limping
to benches adhere
                    fly-fingerers   scab-scratchers
                    ear-and-nose diggers

the entrance   heavy wire over windows   laced with fingers
        and always the loud locks

            DOUBLE JANGLE BANG   they are coming
            DOUBLE JANGLE BANG   they are in
            DOUBLE JANGLE BANG   they move on
            DOUBLE JANGLE BANG   they are gone

                but they have left   something
                        a nine-year-old-boy
he sees vistas of soiled men
                        nobody from Turkey Neck
                                    no kin of his

but the doctor said no   they wouldn't beat him none

a sour bulk   eyes brimful of pus   beckons him over
     feels his threadbare
     jeans and up the T-shirt

and the child says loudly   you know why I done it?
he shamed my girl   pull her li'l panties down
two men guffaw

     you know how I kill him? he goes on
     jes' kneel my knee
     on his little neck
     under the water

Almost

Under the almost deserted boardwalk
the sand had lost its daytime warmth.
She fingered the little welt of corduroy
cut off above his bony knee.
He lifted her hand to that forbidden zone
where his sex stirred like a captive creature
and they were both silent, too young
to know what to say or do.

In the cool sand they turned to each other
smelling cleanly of soap and popcorn
and their arms bound them together like timbers
for a raft and they rocked a little, as if on water.
Her knee pressed where her hand had been
and he groaned a little and their mouths met
in a strange dialogue without words.
Small quiet waves throbbed ashore
and her heart against his torn T-shirt.

He rolled away, his voice breaking,
"Let's run along the water's edge."

He was a little older than she—
a little wiser. And so they ran,
their sandy fingers locked together,
their bare feet pounding on the wet sand,
the splintery boardwalk steps, the road
back to the casino lights and music.
He and his folks would leave tomorrow.
She had two days still to dream.

Wild Ride

Tearing along the Kentucky River road
in a rumble seat, your mouth on mine,
your Swanee College friend, our drunken driver,
and his languid New Orleans girlfriend.
Her soft hand into his thigh, I guessed,
so the car jerked off the road and back on again,
and the wind somehow indecent and unkind
disheveled me and my clothing
or was that your hand that I loved gentle
but now as a paw of this nighttime madness
in the back seat of a roadster that threw us about
like a tin can in surf and I thought,
caught between desire and despair
was it for this was it only for this?

Strays

It started with the cat, a hungry stray.
I fed her, and she made me let her stay.
Soon she was pregnant; and what could I do?
I didn't want a cat and kittens too.
I put their box outside, just past their blindness,
and made a sign: These kittens need your kindness.
I had the females neutered, paying double,
to save the cat and me from further trouble.

A girl came by and knelt beside the box,
all gray: her jacket, jeans, and tennis socks.
She said, "To be unwanted is so sad.
I'd take one, but my father would be mad.
I fed a puppy once, outside.
My father came and kicked it till it died.
And then he threatened me because I cried."

The kittens gone, a few days after that,
she came inside to pet the mother cat.
"I think she's lonely." But she said, "Oh, no,
mothers are glad to see their children go."

Working all night and sleeping all the day,
I watched for June and wanted her to stay.

It looked like rain, one summer afternoon.
The girl looked sad, "I must be going soon."
She laid her cheek against my jacket sleeve.
"You are my husband when I make believe."
I would not do this trusting being harm,
but she turned woman in my circling arm.
She'd asked one time if I had wife and kids.
No, at that time my life was on the skids.
She said, "If I were yours, I'd never leave."
I took her in my arms, "You mustn't grieve."
Flooding the darkened, swiftly emptied streets,
the threatening rain came down in heavy sheets.
I gave her only once a tiny pain:
the price of entry to our love's domain.
We were two lonely persons, well aware
that hate and selfishness are everywhere.
I must have known it would be ending soon,
but for us both it meant a honeymoon.
Where is she now, her parents will not say.
For every inch of heaven, hell to pay;
does kindness always end in bars and chains?
In what we did was nothing cruel or dirty.
The social worker said, "The fact remains
that she was under twelve and you were thirty."

3

Other Loves

The Gardens

They wandered through the gardens, side by side,
down little curving lanes and pathways straight,
with ample lawns and statues. The hour grew late.
What was it that they sought? She could not hide
dismay before a thicket that denied
them passage. Beyond the thorns she saw a gate—
to paradise? He said, "Not now, we'll wait
to see it in the sun," and she complied.

She felt despair, although with walking spent,
to turn away, retrace the homeward maze
leaving unseen that which the half-light lent
a strange enchantment. Never later days
could bring them there again; the paths were blind,
and they had missed what long they searched to find.

Leaves and Snow

The day we danced all day
wherever we found music
we were followed
by a thousand bright leaves
cutting loose
thumbing rides in air
from honey noon
to a mandarin sunset
to cold mists
circling streetlights
to the black porches
of what now.

The night it snowed
and you stayed
before the plow came
you had to walk away
from our bed of summer
across the huge whiteness
     printing
         printing
your dark flowers.

The day of the icicles
when we made love
on the floor
in the winter dazzle
sunfire melting
us together
forced the crystal phallus
by the window
to drop tender
beads
of spring light.

The Burning Ash

Our children run wild beside the wild water:
mine and his, yours and hers. We sit
before the fire in silence in the rough cottage.

The great log gives itself to the flames.
The blessed spirits of the fire
cast their warmth before us, dancing,

dancing to the music of the turning disk
while our children run wild by the tidal river.
You break our silence, saying,

"Is what you feel for me agapé or eros?"
and the great log lets fall a blazing fragment of itself
and the flames dance back and forth, sighing.

The music ends and the disk keeps turning
I am the burning fire, the turning disk, the wild water,
and I cannot find words for an answer.

Following

Someone is always falling in love with you:
men and women, infants and children,
octogenarians and adolescents.
A tenant of heaven-haven on the pearly doorstep
hopes you will wave your hand in passing.
Where you stood just now a white bird
has flown into a ponderosa pine
and a black bee hovers in a bush of yellow flowers.

People would like to discuss you, but hold back.
Mystery is a fragile substance, too easy to tear.
Several persons, however, have noticed that you are followed
not by the usual shadow but by a shaft of sunlight.
Even on a day of fog or light rain.
Even after sunset.

When you are not present, you still walk quietly
through our minds, and we tell ourselves little stories
or small poems about you, like this one.
When a bird sings, we listen carefully
hoping your name will be mentioned.

Sky-Fall

With snow and roses from the skies
the ground is laid for lovers' feet.
What is the substance of their ties?

Still tug my heart with strange surprise
and slow my passage down the street
your snow and roses from the skies.

Once in the mirror of your eyes
this furrowed face was live and sweet.
What was the substance of those ties?

We make no claim and ask no prize
for constancy the years repeat
like snow and roses from the skies.

Physicians of the mind advise
"Brush off the ash of ancient heat;
there is no substance in such ties."

What ending can the gods devise
for lives that touch and never meet?
What is the substance of our ties
but snow and roses from the skies?

You and You

New forms and faces make their mark
in my impenetrable dark.
What in a disembodied ghost
can make me love some more than most?

I'm happy when alone, it's true,
but how much happier with you, and you.
So many I would welcome, if they came,
but keep returning to a certain name . . .

Botticelli's Venus

Love, that soul, fettered to the body, craves,
comes on her fluted shell across the waves.
In dreams her presence fires each lover's heart,
until the jealous daylight makes them part.
But Botticelli lets the lovers dwell
forever watching for the fluted shell.

4

DGA

Religio Amoris

Not in seclusion, down upon my knees;
nor in the crowded hush of holy halls
where spirit chafes as ritual recalls
those outworn emblems, cup and staff and keys;
not from communal chant or lonely pleas
when the poor self or too-rich custom palls
at last, is worship consummate. Still falls
the world about my ears.

    But hours like these,
alone with you in love's communion, bring
a luminous faith, unbridled and unbroken,
freed from neglect and shadow of despair.
I feel that nameless presence where we cling
equivalent to the mystic word unspoken,
doubt's most profound denial, love's deepest prayer.

Task for Two

I pull it toward me
and you turn and lay
it with care and stretch
from marshy verdure drawn
a strong and malleable
stuff repeating a certain
rhythm: our arms tense
but not our mood; we like
doing this together: tighter
you say and I obey you
while the act takes form
between us until we come
close to the finish of that
strand and turn the smooth
frame over, four legs
in air, proud of our under-
side as well as surfaces,
who grow in skill, skill
and the pattern firmer every
time we repeat this ritual
with long and knotted rushes

to reseat a chair together
for the bottoms
of each other, children, friends.

The Sleeping Bag

Feathers and down, down
of our double bag enfold us
in the winter night.

This warmth had wings once
crossing the moon.

One candle at our heads
as for a wake.
One downy feather trembling
in your dark hair.

Your hands over my ears
hold off the buoy bell
the pistol crack of ice.

Wind through our flapping tent
blows out the candle
tugs at guy ropes
makes the trees cry out.

Silence the wind,
deafen me with love, love
in the winged darkness
of down, down.

Waterways

Bayous of Louisiana,
channels between islands of Georgian Bay,
canals of the English midlands,
the butty boat moving silently
in the great summers of our love:

a hundred waterways
within the walls of this darkened room
come and go like beads of light
flashing from a lifted paddle,

floating back our youth between the parted banks
like a water lily
or a vole swimming across the stream.

The Jesting Clouds

Beside a sea that fell like splintered glass
we shared the golden rapture of the sun,
I, smiling at the grains of sand that spun
between my fingers, while a radiant mass
of those great argosies of cloud that pass
across the heavens was mirrored in your eyes.
"If we could get to them, we'd roam the skies,"
you said. A shadow swept the pale dune grass.

Why did you wish for joys beyond our reach?
By some uncalculated sky-born joke
the clouds came down to us on ropes of rain.
We had to race for shelter up the beach,
our luminous sea and sky gone gray as smoke
and the sand sodden where our love had lain.

Fire in the Sandbox

With my favorite playmate, my husband of thirty years,
I came often to our little homestead we named Shiloh
in the vast sandbox of a Mojave valley.
Five acres without roads or wires or water,
but splendid with raw oysters and icy martinis.

Once we saw a faint red glow in the sky
between sunset and gegenschein.
Something to drive toward in the dusk.
Three miles by sand, two or three by road,
and yes the Twenty-nine Palms dump is burning.
Finally we come upon it, a lonely bonfire for our eyes alone.
Beside the shapeless mountain, crest afire,
an abandoned sofa waits in its cretonne cover,
expectant, somehow. "Sit there," I say, and you sit.
"Oh, for a camera and a bit more light,
to have you pose forever on the faded chintz."
Above you on the pinnacle a smoldering baby carriage catches
        fire,
slowly cascading down the cluttered slope.
Why do I see Paolo and Francesca circling the pyre?

Come to my arms, Paolo, before the burning carriage
reaches the sofa.

The tower like Pisa starts to lean,
the bed of flowers no longer green,
the baby carriage in between.

What was the portent of this eerie scene?
Long lost, except in the camera of the mind.
Carrying in our hearts the lovers' flame,
toward Shiloh then we turned and came
while in the dark the sandbox burned.

Bonfire

The flowers in the fields of night
are fading in the coming light.
Their shining petals, one by one,
the winds of day have swept away
into the bonfire of the sun.

5

Love/Death

The Passage

Since you chose to die
I must speak to the dark

A rill of words
insisting on passage

Through the mausoleum of earth
through the zeros of absence

Through choked channels, dry deltas,
into the unanswering sky.

Song for Seven*

For many a spring I watched the buds unfold.
First love, your fifteenth summer was your last.
the leaves fly earthward, and the earth is cold.

Tristan, I was both sister and Isolde.
Letters and poems across the years amassed.
For many a spring I watched the buds unfold.

My best beloved, my heart, how could I hold
one who was living in his country's past?
The leaves fly earthward, and the earth is cold.

The truth of suicide is never told.
Four I held dear called death, and death came fast.
For many a spring I watched the buds unfold.

I was the sheep that sought a shepherd's fold,
he in the amorous role of Jesus cast.
The leaves fly earthward, and the earth is cold.

True Shepherd, lead, for I am blind and old.
The life so bound, desires and dreams so vast.
For many a year I watched the buds unfold,
the leaves fly earthward. And the earth is cold.

*S.A., L.B., D.A., J.J., E.C., A.W., K.J.

Elegy in Fire

His telling glorified her death,
a triumph for the end of breath.
A burning river through them coursed,
drowning the fears that pain endorsed.

See what a fire within them rolls:
volcanoes rise from fumaroles
filling the midnight sky with flames,
fusing together deathless names.

The pure eruption in their blood
was like the lava's living flood.
The silences in flesh and bone
with time would harden into stone.

Pale smoke arising like a wraith
danced at the altar of their faith.
From lives like theirs great legends grow.
The tides that turn, the winds that blow,

the clouds that shed white plumes of snow
repeat the truth for which we yearn,
the truth for which our bodies burn
and silent listeners discern.

First Light

Great flower of fire, whose petals never fall,
your garden has no gateway, path, or wall.
At times you vanish in a cloud so black
it takes my prayers and tears to bring you back.
Your fragrance fills my soul, from grief withdrawn,
O, flower of fire, my waking and my dawn.

Sun God

How beautiful your burning need
to resurrect the buried seed
and reaffirm your glorious power
to let the bud become a flower.

PART IV

MINDSIGHT

Abundance

From mountain summits that I cannot see,
the wind has brought the taste of snow to me
and night returns me, with a breath of frost,
the rim of white on Baldy, nine years lost.

Blind to abundance when I was not blind,
I breathe one rose and hold it in my mind.

Only These

Only the deaf hear music purified of words,
tuned to their heartbeat, trembling flesh and bone.

Only the blind see airy beings in lamplight or sunray
sailing across a summer sea,
where the walls of a room go down like Jericho.

Only the paralyzed race so freely
back through the meadows of time to the old homestead
with its porches facing the blue hills.

The Sound of Sunlight

This simple pleasure never can take place:
to see your eyes, the contours of your face.
I am not certain if you sit or stand,
but twice have felt the firmness of your hand.

In company, yours is the voice I turn for,
carrying the vanished sunlight that I yearn for.
Then, when you leave, I guess the good-bye smile,
and part of you stays with me for a while.

Cloud of Unseeing

Sightless,
I have become a stranger to my own person.
Whose are these fingers, now indifferent to a book, a letter?

Print has nothing to say to them.
Primitives, that push pages aside
though they will fondle a stone, feel around the plate
for a bean, a crust, a piece of fruit.

They glide over a mirror, uncomprehending.
They seem to remember that once
a face lived there, like an owl
peering from a hole in a tree.

But a tree is now a rough column to bump into.
An invisible mockingbird is a watchman,
telling me of the night, suggesting it is safe
to go on dream journeys

where sometimes shapes reappear
like the pair of scissors, not long ago,

or a whole scenario, as in the old days
before the world of shapes and colors ended
and my fingers became puzzling parts
of a creature I can barely imagine.

The Last Dawn

I rose and balanced with my cane.
When would the daylight come again?
The desert air was pure and cold.
Strange to be blind and deaf and old.
Where was our little desert shack,
the two-hole privy at the back?
The ring of mountains, high and stark?
Our land had vanished in the dark.

Then, beacon to my pinprick eye,
a strange fire in the eastern sky
across the lost hill deeply spread:
within the black, a burning red.

I stand in silent ecstasy:
a final dawn is granted me.

Navigating by Night

I remember steering after dark
in the treacherous channels of Georgian Bay
between islands, all those summers ago,
watching the pieces of paler sky,
among darker patterns of tree and rock.

Now in this inland valley, they tell me it is daylight
but again, I move between dark islands.
I seek direction in the paleness overhead,
as when formerly all days came in color—
indigo water, conifer green, granite pink—
where water mirrored the rocky shore,
the red canoes, the fish leaping for flies at sundown:
scenes that come now only in sleep and memory,
the boat moving soundlessly, steering by the sky,
along dark channels of the mind.

Filling the Pages

When I was two, I drew.
The pictures went wild in my head
and onto the page, wherever the crayon led.
"What's that?"
"It's Muvver in her big hat."

At three I could read and write
letters and numbers, but not spell.
My notebook pages were white.
My father dated the notebooks;
I filled one. Started another.

I wanted a brother, but he never came.
I drew mostly boys, no one I knew.
I would talk to them and laugh as I drew.

Now it has been six years since I saw
anything much, but I still want to draw,
to get back the wonderful touch, when
I picked up the pencil or pen.

The children still run streaming out of my mind,
only now I am blind; and it's so queer
at this stage they can no longer appear
on the white page.

Having It All

To complain now is heresy, but I am haunted
by a voice reading the story of Ulysses.
My shores are shaken by the sea.
The sun entered my room this morning
like an old lover returning from some far place.
What do I wish, at my age? The lifelong hunger
to run on hard sand, to lie again
in warm arms, whispering and laughing.
I have had it all and want it back again,
when mornings like this fill my black cave
with seductive sunlight.

But to complain is heresy, to yearn for beaches, foolish.
Perhaps I should have drowned young
on that terrible afternoon off the Nag's Head coast—
my little children playing with their pails and shovels,
their father coming for the weekend;
he would have found a new mother for them,
a new woman for himself.
I was spared, for another lifetime beside a different sea.

The western ocean is a stranger, beautiful and alien.
Perhaps oceans are all one, but not to me.

I will run my tub in the darkness,
lie there in the warm water, my invisible self
rocking and slipping between gratitude and longing,
with only a taped voice to return to,
telling of the restless, all-demanding sea,
the adventures of Ulysses.

I am not entirely old, and to complain is heresy.

Listening

On the margin of sleep
I am talking to myself
in silence, silence.

I read the transcription
strung out in seaweed
which the waves shuffle and erase.

My thumb stirring
under the pillow
sounds like footsteps.

But no one comes
only the words walking
connecting and recombining.

A shadowy poem joins them
and I come awake quickly
to catch what it is saying.

My senses tremble
but the poem is untranslatable
with runic gestures pointing

to silence, silence.

Thresholds

I stand at evening in the open door,
and see the wind I never saw before.

Freed from the restless eyes I've left behind,
I move through endless galleries of the mind.

Lord, as I cross the threshold into light,
pray keep my soul and give me back my sight.

PART V

SAND GARDENS

Envoys

Our varied envoys to Japan
taught it the power of Christian man.
The Japanese were willing then
to teach us martial arts and Zen,
to eat raw fish, and understand
gardens made of rocks and sand.

Transfer

I move from vistas carved in light
to shadows darkening into night
where water listens in a bowl
to sounds of sea and sun and soul.

Welcome Wind

Now on the brink of afternoon, the wind
out of the far west is due to arrive
from the crash of waves bringing a taste of salt,
a hint of wet sea sand.

Leaving the coast, this welcome wind
careens over the shoreline cities
heading for the hills and canyons,
turning the cottonwood leaves inside out,
puzzling the rare cloud on its way to the sunset.

All this, a prelude, an evening canticle, the heart sings
after a hot day, to the punctual wind from the ocean,
enveloping us in its great cloak of air,
playing with the birds, teasing us into poems.

Mojave Sunset

When the afternoon wind arrives from the sea
the blue tent of the sky flaps open in welcome,
the sands dance in long cotillions
and the jackrabbit leaps from its hiding place
under the flowering creosote.
At the eastern end of Wonder Valley
the long pale hill of sand turns to rose
in the final rays of the sun.
To the north, the Sheephole Mountain
begins its preparations for the cool evening,
long purple robes trailing down the arroyos.
As the sky dims into dusk, the vast garden of the valley
blooms with stars, and our hands with gratitude
touch the quiet stones, the cooling sand.

Loving Stones

In the Mojave, east of here,
the wind talks to the stones
and they whisper back.

We say "stone cold," "stone dead,"
yet the sun embraces them,
the moon finds them beautiful,
clouds drape their shadows over these stones.

Every wind-honed rock tells the story of the earth,
its hot core, its cold seas,
recites the sagas of riverbeds
where they once lay or tumbled.
Learning patience. Achieving grace.

The Boulder

This was the rock
where the last eagle's farsighted gaze
from this height
beheld the first wagon train
coming from the desert to the sea,
preceding the planters and the smog.

And when the eagle
melted into the sky and was gone
smaller birds knew the boulder
for a holy place.

Unlike the lesser stones of the mountain
it will not loosen in the darkside ice
or relax in the summer rain.
It will not rumble, tumble, crumble.

Remember its silence
in a long night when sleep will not come.
Remember it in the long sleep

when the rare flowers come up
through the grains of sand around our bones
and the ghostly eagle carries away the sun.

Then

Then I could run forever on the beach,
the sun, the sea, the world within my reach.
My parents beckoned from a soundless height;
their shadows lengthened in the failing light,
and all at once I feared the coming night.

Some Night

Some night the ocean wind will take my hand,
and lead me to his garden in the sand:
no fruit to gather, no sweet flower to smell,
only a gull's feather and a broken shell.

Notes

An Hour in Aldwinkle: brass-rubbers and churchgoers will know what is meant; at this time, most small towns had a pub near the church.

Hard to Die: see the journal of Meriwether Lewis.

The Great River: Anderson Gratz ("Uncle Andy"), who married a cousin from our family, had the 120-foot *Polly* built with a shallow draft that enabled it to sail in two feet of water. He had the candy and baseballs wrapped in oiled paper in such a way that they would float (the peppermint sticks weighed almost half a pound).

The Sound of Progress: all resemblances to "God's Grandeur" by Gerard Manley Hopkins are, of course, intentional.

Echoes: see T. S. Eliot's "The Waste Land," which refers to Phlebas the Phoenician.

Hetaera McMurdo: in the 1930s, my father bought the McMurdo Silver Masterpiece, a large combination radio/record player, a machine ahead of its time. It played a record uninterruptedly for around half an hour. It had several speeds and could also change records automatically, sliding them down a felt-covered incline. *Hetaera* was the ancient Greek term for courtesan or mistress.

The Caller: This story poem is based on Barbara McBeth's account of her Sunday afternoon drives as a child with her grandmother.

Sky-Fall: this villanelle bases its imagery upon a bouquet of roses being thrown through a basement apartment window by a lover on a snowy day.

Botticelli's Venus: inspired by the famous painting *The Birth of Venus.*

DGA: my husband, Douglass Graybill Adair.

Waterways: on canal boat trips in the English Midlands, the butty boat, having no engine but with cabins for about eight passengers, was pulled by a motorboat that had a dining room and a small crew.

Elegy in Fire: an irrational rhapsody composed without plan or pause, but somehow nudged into being by the spoken elegy of a bereaved husband.

Having It All: listening to a reading of the Ulysses epic, on tape, from the Braille Library.

Acknowledgments

Connie Kimos, for the many ways she supported me in the production of this manuscript

Members of the fortnightly poetry group, founded by Marcyn del Clements and Mike Ranney

Judy Casanova, for her help with my revisions

And always, Bob Mezey

VIRGINIA HAMILTON ADAIR was born in 1913 in New York City. She taught briefly at the University of Wisconsin, the College of William & Mary, and Pomona College, and for many years at California Polytechnic University at Pomona. She was recently awarded an honorary doctorate from her alma mater, Mount Holyoke.

ABOUT THE TYPE

This book was set in Garamond, a typeface originally designed by the Parisian typecutter Claude Garamond (1480–1561). This version of Garamond was modeled on a 1592 specimen sheet from the Egenolff-Berner foundry, which was produced from types assumed to have been brought to Frankfurt by the punchcutter Jacques Sabon.

Claude Garamond's distinguished romans and italics first appeared in *Opera Ciceronis* in 1543–44. The Garamond types are clear, open, and elegant.